Civil War Recipes

Adding and Subtracting Simple Fractions

Lynn George

PowerMath™

New Hanover County Public Library
201 Chestnut Street
Wilmington, NC 28401

The recipes in this cookbook are intended for a child
to make together with an adult.

Published in 2004 by The Rosen Publishing Group, Inc.
29 East 21st Street, New York, NY 10010

Book Design: Ron A. Churley

Photo Credits: Cover, p. 6 © Bettmann/Corbis; pp. 9, 10, 17, 18, 22 © Corbis; p. 14 © Michelle
Garrett/Corbis; p. 15 © Medford Historical Society Collection/Corbis.

Library of Congress Cataloging-in-Publication Data

George, Lynn.
  Civil War recipes : adding and subtracting simple fractions / Lynn
George.
      p. cm. — (PowerMath)
Includes index.
Summary: Gives several examples of recipes used during the Civil War,
such as gingerbread, groundnut soup, gumbo, and hardtack, and shows how
to add and subtract fractions to double or halve the ingredients.
  ISBN 0-8239-8973-9 (lib. bdg.)
  ISBN 0-8239-8896-1 (pbk.)
  6-pack ISBN: 0-8239-7424-3
  1. Fractions—Juvenile literature. 2. Recipes—United
States—Juvenile literature. [1. Fractions. 2. Recipes. 3. Cookery,
American—History—19th century.] I. Title. II. Series.
  QA117.G46 2004
  513.2'6—dc21
                              2002153793

Manufactured in the United States of America

Contents

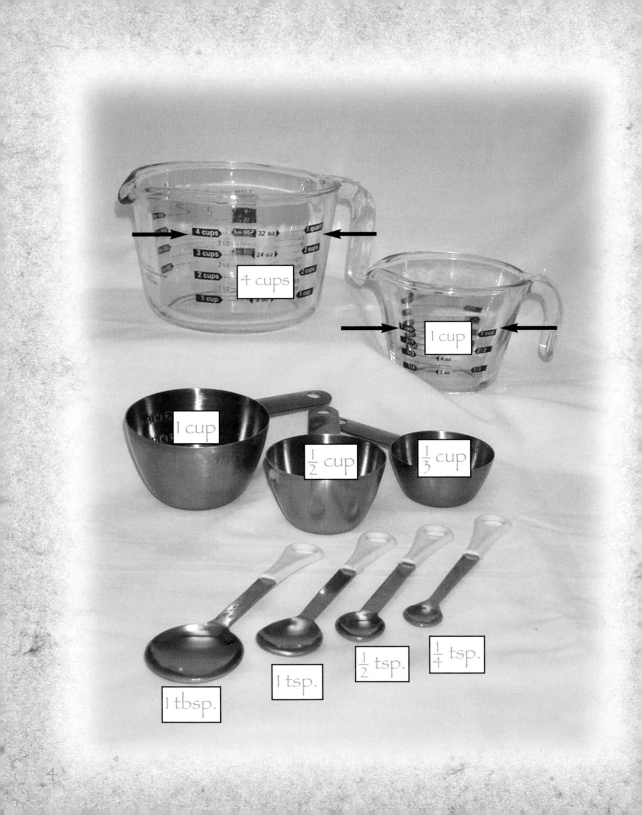

4 cups

1 cup

1 cup

½ cup

⅓ cup

1 tsp.

½ tsp.

¼ tsp.

1 tbsp.

4

Math for Cooks

Have you ever helped prepare one of your favorite foods? Did you realize you were using math? In fact, you couldn't cook without math! Recipes use standard measurements like cups, tablespoons, and teaspoons to tell you how much of each **ingredient** you need. That's math!

Most recipes also have measurements that include fractions. You need to know how to add and subtract fractions if you want to change a recipe to feed more people or fewer people. To add and subtract fractions, you need to know that there are several different, but equal, ways to write each fraction. For example, $\frac{1}{2} = \frac{2}{4} = \frac{4}{8}$, and $\frac{1}{4} = \frac{2}{8}$. Let's look at the recipe on the following pages to see how to increase a recipe to feed more people.

Recipes often use short forms for standard measurements instead of writing out the complete words. Here are short forms for some common measurements: lb. = pound, qt. = quart, tbsp. = tablespoon, tsp. = teaspoon.

The gingerbread recipe on page 7 gives us a peek into the past. It came from a girl named Josephine Peffer, who lived in Wisconsin in 1860. Josephine won a blue ribbon for her gingerbread at the 1860 Wisconsin State Fair.

Gingerbread

You Will Need:

1 cup **molasses**

$\frac{1}{4}$ lb. butter, softened

$\frac{1}{2}$ cup buttermilk

2 eggs

1 tbsp. ginger

1 tsp. baking powder

2 cups flour

How to Do It:

Preheat the oven to 350°F. Butter a 9-inch square pan and dust it lightly with flour. Beat the $\frac{1}{4}$ pound of butter until it is smooth and creamy.* Add the eggs and beat well. Add the buttermilk and molasses, and blend. In a separate bowl, mix together the flour, ginger, and baking powder. Add the flour mixture to the butter mixture and mix well. Pour the batter into the pan and bake for 35 minutes. Stick a toothpick into the center of the gingerbread. If it comes out clean, the gingerbread is done. If it doesn't, bake the gingerbread for about 10 more minutes. Cool in the pan, then cut into 9 pieces. Serves 9.

*You can use an electric mixer, even though such mixers did not exist in Josephine's day.

Suppose you wanted to make enough of Josephine's gingerbread for 18 people. You would need to make 2 pans of gingerbread. How much of the ingredients would you need? Double all of the ingredients to find out.

When you double a recipe, that means you add an equal amount of each ingredient. If a recipe calls for $\frac{1}{3}$ cup of something, you add another $\frac{1}{3}$ cup for a total of $\frac{2}{3}$ cup.

Gingerbread
(double recipe)

You Will Need:

Molasses: 1 cup + 1 cup = 2 cups

Ginger: 1 tbsp. + 1 tbsp. = 2 tbsps.

Butter: $\frac{1}{4}$ lb. + $\frac{1}{4}$ lb. = $\frac{2}{4}$ lb. = $\frac{1}{2}$ lb.

Baking powder: 1 tsp. + 1 tsp. = 2 tsps.

Buttermilk: $\frac{1}{2}$ cup + $\frac{1}{2}$ cup = 1 cup

Flour: 2 cups + 2 cups = 4 cups

Eggs: 2 eggs + 2 eggs = 4 eggs

The American Civil War

We can use recipes and math skills to learn more about the time in which Josephine lived. In 1861, just a year after Josephine won a blue ribbon for her gingerbread recipe, the **American Civil War** started. It lasted until 1865. This war was caused by disagreements between the Northern states and the Southern states about how to run the country. One of the biggest arguments was about slavery. The owners of large **plantations** in the South used slaves to raise and harvest the crops. These slaves were adults and children who had been taken by force from their homes in Africa. Many Northerners knew that slavery was wrong and wanted to end it.

African Slaves and Their Foods

Slaves were given very little food. Their main food was **cornmeal**. They could mix the cornmeal with water or buttermilk and fry it in a pan to make a simple bread.

Some slaves brought with them seeds for foods they had eaten in Africa. They grew these foods on small plots of land the plantation owners allowed them to use. Some of the foods they brought to the United States became important parts of American meals. One of these foods is the peanut, which is sometimes called a "goober" in the South. The word "goober" comes from the African word for peanut, "*nguba.*" "*Nguba*" actually means "groundnut." Africans used peanuts to make a healthy soup.

Groundnut Soup

You Will Need:

2 tbsps. oil

1 onion, chopped

2 cloves of garlic, finely chopped

1 tomato, chopped

$\frac{2}{3}$ cup paste made of
   crushed peanuts (or use $\frac{2}{3}$ cup
   creamy peanut butter)*

$\frac{1}{4}$ tsp. red (cayenne) pepper

$\frac{1}{2}$ tsp. ginger

4 cups chicken or
   vegetable broth

salt and pepper (add a little
   at a time until it tastes good)

How to Do It:

* Before preparing this recipe, make sure no one is allergic to peanuts.

Heat the oil in a large pan over medium-low heat. Add the chopped onion. Cook and stir for 5 minutes. Add the chopped garlic. Cook and stir for 1 more minute. Add the chopped tomato, peanut butter, red pepper, ginger, and 6 tablespoons of the chicken (or vegetable) broth. Stir until ingredients form a smooth paste. Add the remaining broth slowly, stirring constantly, until mixture forms a smooth soup. Cover the pan and simmer the soup over medium-low heat for 10 minutes. Remove the lid and simmer uncovered for 10 to 15 minutes. Add salt and pepper a little at a time until the soup tastes good. Serve hot. Serves 6.

How much of the ingredients would you need if you wanted to prepare this soup for only 3 people? To find out, reduce all of the ingredients by half. When you cut a recipe in half, that means you are subtracting half the amount of each ingredient.

Groundnut Soup
(half recipe)

Oil: 2 tbsps. − 1 tbsp. = 1 tbsp.

Onion: 1 onion − $\frac{1}{2}$ onion = $\frac{1}{2}$ onion

Garlic: 2 cloves − 1 clove = 1 clove

Tomato: 1 tomato − $\frac{1}{2}$ tomato = $\frac{1}{2}$ tomato

Peanut butter: $\frac{2}{3}$ cup − $\frac{1}{3}$ cup = $\frac{1}{3}$ cup

Red pepper: $\frac{1}{4}$ tsp. = $\frac{2}{8}$ tsp.

$\frac{2}{8}$ tsp. − $\frac{1}{8}$ tsp. = $\frac{1}{8}$ tsp.

Ginger: $\frac{1}{2}$ tsp. = $\frac{2}{4}$ tsp.

$\frac{2}{4}$ tsp. − $\frac{1}{4}$ tsp. = $\frac{1}{4}$ tsp.

Chicken or vegetable broth: 4 cups − 2 cups = 2 cups

African slaves also brought seeds for the **okra** plant with them. Okra was used to make a thick soup called "gumbo." This name comes from the African word for okra, which is "*nkombo*." Gumbo is still popular in the southern United States today.

Gumbo

You Will Need:

4 cups okra, sliced
8 cups tomatoes, chopped
3 lbs. chicken, cut into pieces
5 qts. water

1 tsp. red (cayenne) pepper
salt (add a little at a time until
   it tastes good)

How to Do It:

Put 5 quarts of water in a large soup pot. Add the chicken pieces and simmer uncovered for 2 hours. Add okra, tomatoes, and red pepper. Simmer uncovered for 2 more hours. Add salt a little at a time until it tastes good. Serve hot with cooked rice. Serves 12.

You probably wouldn't want to make this full recipe, since it serves 12 people. How much of the ingredients would you need if you wanted to make enough for 6 people? Since 6 is half of 12, you can reduce all of the ingredients by half.

Gumbo
(half recipe)

You Will Need:

Okra: 4 cups − 2 cups = 2 cups

Tomatoes: 8 cups − 4 cups = 4 cups

Chicken: 3 lbs. − $1\frac{1}{2}$ lbs. = $1\frac{1}{2}$ lbs.

Water: 5 qts. − $2\frac{1}{2}$ qts. = $2\frac{1}{2}$ qts.

Red pepper: 1 tsp. − $\frac{1}{2}$ tsp. = $\frac{1}{2}$ tsp.

okra

Soldiers and Their Foods

The peanuts introduced by African slaves formed an important part of the soldiers' meals during the Civil War. Soldiers ate peanuts plain and also used them in cooking. Both Northern and Southern soldiers made a peanut soup, though it was much simpler than African groundnut soup. They boiled peanuts in water and added a little ham for extra flavor. There was no real recipe for this soup. The amount of peanuts and ham the soldiers used depended on how much they had.

Cornbread was an important food for Southern soldiers. Sometimes they made a simple cornbread called "sagamite." It had only 2 ingredients— cornmeal and brown sugar— which were mixed together and baked in a pan over a fire.

Northern soldiers ate bread that was called "hardtack" because it was so hard and dry. In fact, soldiers called their squares of hardtack "tooth dullers" or "sheet iron crackers." The hardtack was baked in Northern factories and often took months to reach the soldiers, who were far away.

Hardtack

You Will Need:

$\frac{1}{3}$ cup water   1 cup flour

$\frac{1}{2}$ tbsp. salt

How to Do It:

Preheat the oven to 375°F. Mix all the ingredients in a bowl to make a stiff batter. Sprinkle some flour on the table. Take the batter out of the bowl and put it on the table. Use your fingers to pat the stiff batter into a square that is about 6 inches on each side and about $\frac{1}{2}$ inch thick. Cut into four 3-inch squares. In each square, punch 4 rows of holes, with 4 holes in each row. Put squares onto a baking sheet. Bake for 45 minutes. Cool the hardtack on wire racks before eating. Makes 4 squares.

How much of the ingredients would you need to make 8 hardtack squares instead of 4? To find out, double all of the ingredients.

Hardtack
(double recipe)

You Will Need:

Water: $\frac{1}{3}$ cup + $\frac{1}{3}$ cup = $\frac{2}{3}$ cup

Salt: $\frac{1}{2}$ tbsp. + $\frac{1}{2}$ tbsp. = 1 tbsp.

Flour: 1 cup + 1 cup = 2 cups

This hardtack was made in 1864!

What Civilians Ate

Very soon after the Civil War started, **civilians** in the South began to have problems getting enough food. Slaves ran away, and there were not enough people to work on the plantations. Also, there were not many trains in the South, so it was hard to move food from the plantations where it was grown to the battlefields where it was needed. Even basic foods like flour, sugar, salt, eggs, and butter were hard to get. Here's a recipe for cornbread from a cookbook published in Richmond, Virginia, in 1863. Because it calls for buttermilk, flour, and molasses, some people would not have been able to get the ingredients to make it.

Richmond near the end of the Civil War

Cornbread

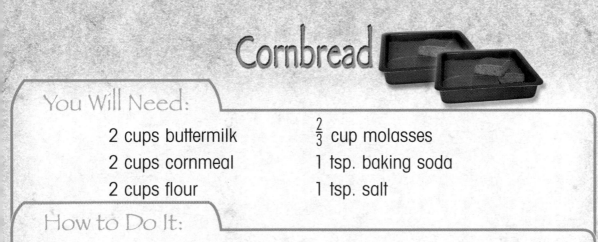

You Will Need:

2 cups buttermilk

2 cups cornmeal

2 cups flour

$\frac{2}{3}$ cup molasses

1 tsp. baking soda

1 tsp. salt

How to Do It:

Preheat the oven to 425°F. Grease two 9-inch square pans. In a large bowl, mix cornmeal, flour, baking soda, and salt. Add the buttermilk and molasses, and mix well. Pour into the pans and bake for 15 to 20 minutes. Cool, then cut the cornbread in each pan into 9 squares. Serves 18.

How much of the ingredients would you need to make just 1 pan (or 9 squares) of cornbread? Reduce all of the ingredients by half to find out.

Half Recipe

You Will Need:

Buttermilk: 2 cups − 1 cup = 1 cup

Cornmeal: 2 cups − 1 cup = 1 cup

Flour: 2 cups − 1 cup = 1 cup

Molasses: $\frac{2}{3}$ cup − $\frac{1}{3}$ cup = $\frac{1}{3}$ cup

Baking soda: 1 tsp. − $\frac{1}{2}$ tsp. = $\frac{1}{2}$ tsp.

Salt: 1 tsp. − $\frac{1}{2}$ tsp. = $\frac{1}{2}$ tsp.

During the Civil War, civilians in the North were usually able to get enough food. Northern farms were still able to raise good crops, and trains quickly carried foods from one place to another. Milk, butter, eggs, sugar, and molasses were not hard to get. Northerners used these ingredients to make things like brown bread.

Northern Brown Bread

You Will Need:

1 tsp. salt

1 tsp. baking soda

$\frac{1}{2}$ cup all-purpose flour

1 egg, beaten

$\frac{1}{3}$ cup molasses

$\frac{1}{3}$ cup brown sugar, packed

1 cup buttermilk

$1\frac{1}{3}$ cups whole wheat flour

How to Do It:

Preheat oven to 300°F. Grease a loaf pan that is $8\frac{1}{2}$ inches by $4\frac{1}{2}$ inches by $2\frac{1}{2}$ inches. Mix together the salt, baking soda, and all-purpose flour. Add all the remaining ingredients. Stir by hand for 5 minutes. Pour batter into the loaf pan. Bake for about 1 hour, or until a toothpick stuck into the center of the bread comes out clean. Carefully take the bread out of the pan and put it on a wire cooling rack. Let the bread cool before slicing. Makes 1 loaf.

How much of the ingredients would you need to make 2 loaves of Northern Brown Bread? To find out, double all of the ingredients.

Northern Brown Bread
(double recipe)

You Will Need:

Salt: 1 tsp. + 1 tsp. = 2 tsps.

Baking soda: 1 tsp. + 1 tsp. = 2 tsps.

All-purpose flour: $\frac{1}{2}$ cup + $\frac{1}{2}$ cup = 1 cup

Eggs: 1 egg + 1 egg = 2 eggs

Molasses: $\frac{1}{3}$ cup + $\frac{1}{3}$ cup = $\frac{2}{3}$ cup

Brown sugar, packed: $\frac{1}{3}$ cup + $\frac{1}{3}$ cup = $\frac{2}{3}$ cup

Buttermilk: 1 cup + 1 cup = 2 cups

Whole wheat flour: $1\frac{1}{3}$ cups + $1\frac{1}{3}$ cups = $2\frac{2}{3}$ cups

After the War

The North recovered quickly after the war. The South did not. Most of the battles had been fought in the South. Cities and plantations had been destroyed. It took many years for life in the South to get better. One of the things that helped to improve the economy of the South was a food introduced by slaves—the peanut.

George Washington Carver, who had been born into slavery in 1864, became a famous scientist. He discovered that growing peanuts added **nutrients** to the soil that made the soil better for growing all kinds of crops. Carver encouraged Southern farmers to plant peanuts. He also invented more than 300 ways to use peanuts, including peanut flour, peanut oil for cooking, and everybody's favorite— peanut butter!

George Washington Carver

Glossary

American Civil War (uh-MAIR-uh-kuhn SIH-vuhl WOHR) A war fought between the Northern and Southern states of the United States from 1861 to 1865.

civilian (suh-VIHL-yuhn) Someone who is not a soldier.

cornmeal (KORN-meel) A coarse flour made by grinding corn.

ingredient (in-GREE-dee-uhnt) Each of the things that are part of a recipe.

molasses (muh-LA-suhz) A thick, sweet, dark syrup that comes from sugarcane.

nutrient (NOO-tree-uhnt) Anything that a living thing needs for energy or to grow.

okra (OH-kruh) A vegetable brought to the United States from Africa.

plantation (plan-TAY-shun) A large cotton, tobacco, or sugarcane farm owned by one family and worked by the people who lived on the land.

Index

ML   6/04